WAG Your work

Writing Accountability Groups

Boot Camp for Increasing Scholarly Productivity

Kimberly A. Skarupski, PhD, MPH

To those about to write...I salute you!

Contents

ACKNOWLEDGMENTS

This book would not have been possible without the inspiration and generosity of the following:

Kharma Foucher, MD, PhD, who originally had the idea to start a writing group in our Research Mentoring Program at Rush University Medical Center in Chicago, IL, and who presented early WAG research outcomes (and got an award for it); Hannah J. Lundberg, PhD, who shared writing tracking tools she developed while in the Rush writing group; Cynthia Rand, PhD, my scathingly brilliant mentor who encouraged me to start WAGs at Johns Hopkins University, School of Medicine; the original WAGGERs at Hopkins: Alicia Arbaje, MD, PhD; Panagis Galiatsatos, MD; Michelle Eakin, PhD; Jin Hui Joo, MD; Jessica Peirce, PhD; Durga Roy, PhD; Ms. Emily Evers; Shari Lawson, MD; Joseph McSharry, Instructional Technologist at Hopkins, who conceived of producing a recorded version of me giving my WAG talk (in a little room with lots of lights and a lone camera) and then provided me with water, encouragement, and a fainting couch in aforementioned little room; Valerie Hartman, MS, Instructional Designer at Hopkins, who took my wordy WAG handout and turned it into a lovely infographic and then gave me great advice to improve this book; Toby Johnson, RA, LEED AP, my BFF, who illustrated the book and also provided sassy advice; Casey Callanan, BS, who encouraged me to self-publish and project-managed the WAG website and marketing plan. Finally, Dana G. Venenga, Colonel (Ret), USAF, MSC, author of *Leadership Secrets of a Slug*, the first person to read and edit the book, and the most encouraging, humble, and loving, Christ-centered man I've ever known.

INTRODUCTION

Writing is hard. In fact, it is agony for most of us. In his awesome book, *How to Write a Lot*, Dr. Paul Silvia (2007) says, "Writing is frustrating, complicated, and un-fun." Writing is even harder when your day is jam-packed with seeing patients, charting, teaching, running research labs and projects, sitting in meetings, attending to various, never-ending administrative, regulatory, and compliance issues, and on and on. Because of this busy-ness, our scholarly writing is oftentimes relegated to midnight hours and weekends. This work-life *dis*integration is not sustainable and may lead to stress and burnout. You want to write; you just don't see *how* to manage it. You need a WAG (writing accountability group).

I have personally started more than 150 WAGs with more than 500 faculty members and trainees (post-docs, residents, and fellows) at Johns Hopkins University, and I've given my WAG talk at many other institutions. When I ask attendees to identify their writing barriers, the top-three troubles always include starting, time, and finishing. WAGs will help you overcome these writing hurdles.

What is a WAG?

A WAG is a peer-led writing group that meets once a week for 10 weeks. A WAG is limited to four to eight members, each of whom must commit to attending at least eight of the ten sessions. WAGs are focused on the *process* of writing with the goal of establishing a sustainable writing habit. WAGs are not focused on the *content* of writing; thus, there is no peer review or editing of your writing.

WAGs follow a strict agenda starting with 15 minutes of updates and goal setting, followed by 30 minutes of communal writing, and then finished by 15 minutes of reporting and wrap-up.

"When performance is measured, performance improves. When performance is measured AND reported, the rate of improvement accelerates"
-Thomas Monson

This principle applies to weight loss (tracking nutrition), exercise (tracking workouts), household budgeting (tracking expenses), and mastering any skill (tracking practice and milestones). In a WAG, the emphasis is on the word *accountability*. Accountability to yourself and to your fellow WAGGERs increases the likelihood that you will achieve your writing goals. The accountability happens via oral reporting and written documentation of your 10-week writing goal(s), your weekly writing goals, and your weekly writing activity and progress.

Why join a WAG instead of just writing on your own? Because "as iron sharpens iron, so one person sharpens another" (Proverbs 27:17). Without a committed writing time and a group to whom we are accountable, many of us simply cannot or just do not make the time to write. And if you're in academia, where scholarship is the currency of the trade, the coin of the realm, writing is your job—so you should be doing your job every day! WAGs will help you grow your scholarly bank account.

The goal of a WAG is to establish a sustainable writing *habit*—writing with increased regularity and for shorter durations, which is sustainable. Even if you have no writing time other than in your WAG, by the end of 10 weeks, at least you will have written for five hours (30 minutes X 10 weeks), which is more writing than many busy academicians, and certainly more than busy clinical academicians, may accomplish.

There are at least three outcomes you will observe by the end of your 10-week WAG: (1) You will find yourself writing with increased regularity and for shorter durations—which is a sustainable writing habit! (2) You will likely experience a newfound sense of confidence, control over the writing process, and satisfaction with your writing practice; and (3) You will also likely experience improved well-being via establishing new friendships and a small community of engagement.

Figure 1 shows writing frequency data from some of our School of Medicine WAGGERs before they started WAGGING (n = 403) and after their first 10 weeks of WAGGING (n = 227). Before starting a WAG, when I ask faculty members how often they write, a little more than a third (36 percent) report once a week, 18 percent say twice a month, and 17 percent say almost every day. After finishing their WAG, when I ask faculty members how often they write, a whopping 68 percent report almost every day!

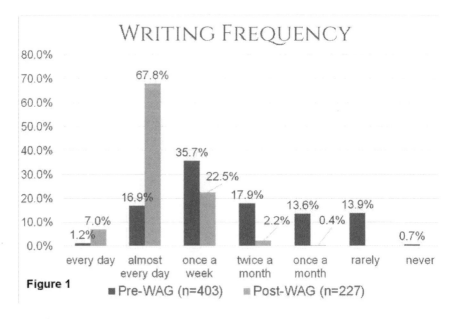

Figure 1

Figure 2 shows the data for writing duration. Before starting a WAG, I also ask faculty members to report the writing duration of their typical writing session. Almost one-third (30 percent) report writing for two or more hours, more than one quarter (26 percent) report writing for one to two hours, and almost one-fifth (16 percent) report writing for 46–60 minutes. See how the post-WAG bars shift to the left? After finishing their WAG, nearly one-quarter report writing for 46–60 minutes (27 percent), 31–45 minutes (24 percent), or 16–30 minutes (23 percent). This is sustainable writing. You may be wondering why there were fewer respondents for those post-WAG data points. I have no evidence of huge dropouts; rather, lots of evidence for survey fatigue, and I don't send follow-up nagging emails.

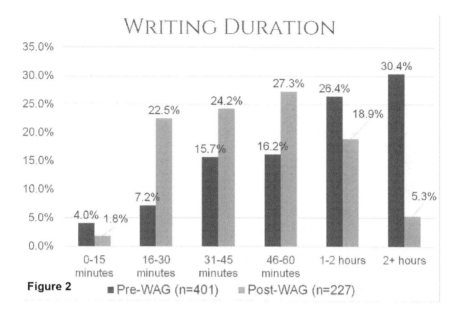

Figure 2

After participating in a WAG, most report feeling a greater sense of control over the writing process (86 percent) and feel like they have better time management (71 percent), and 100 percent agreed with the statement: "My WAG has become a source of social support for me." When I ask WAGGERs what they like best about WAGGING, they report things like accountability, peer support, feedback, a bit of competition, being intentional about writing, liking the structure, dedicated time, and dedication to writing and nothing else. One recently noted: "I enjoy being with my fellow WAGGERs and have established relationships with faculty members I did not previously know." The data are compelling.

WAG mantra: Writing is my job. I will do my job every day.

In the next few chapters, you'll read about common writing myths and barriers. Perhaps you'll recognize some of your own personal writing bugaboos in the next sections. Each chapter will challenge these common writing myths and barriers and will include several recommendations for overcoming those particular hitches in your giddy-up. At the end of each chapter, I've included a section where you can jot down at least three things that you'll start doing, stop doing, and continue doing to establish your own sustainable writing habit. As you read through the chapters, turn to that last page and hold yourself accountable by making a note to self! After that, you'll learn how WAGs work and how to start WAGGING.

CHAPTER *ONE*
The Myth of The Muse

The myth of the muse is one of the most common writing myths. This is the false belief that there's something magical or mysterious about writing. Many of us come up with all kinds of excuses NOT to write— "I can't write because I'm not in the mood." "I don't have my mojo today." "I don't feel inspired." "I'm bloated." "My leg hurts." "I'm tired." "I really need to get to my emails."

We come up with all kinds of excuses for not writing. Funny how we don't use those same excuses for seeing patients or doing surgery! We never call in and say, "I'm really not in the patient-seeing kind of space today. My surgeries? I'm really not feeling it. I kind of feel bloated. I've got this thing in my back, and I just can't concentrate. I'm kind of depressed. I just don't think I'll be able to get to that clinical stuff today." Or, "I'm not going to go to my meeting with a client today because I just feel kind of cranky and I slept funny." "Teaching my course today? Nah . . . maybe next week. They have plenty of time to learn stuff."

Many of us put off our writing as the last possible thing. We'll do anything else before writing. We'll clean behind the refrigerator before we think about writing. Why? Because it's hard. But writing is the same as everything else; it's nothing special. You just have to practice it to get better at it. You got good at performing surgery, teaching, leading project teams, designing quality improvement processes, running, lifting, playing bass, cooking, and speaking Japanese by practice, just like anything else. Writing is just like that!

The muse myth is the idea that there's some tiny, sparkly, writing fairy princess who lives up in the heavens. When she hears us emphatically state: "Now, I shall write!" she flies her bedazzled pixie wings over and showers us with writing fairy dust, trilling: "Yes, yes, write, sweetheart! Write like the wind!" Then, all of a sudden, there's a mystical, swirling vortex of brain cotton candy and we're like, "Whoa! It's happening! I have the power!" The words start spilling out of us like silk and liquid gold, and our brains and our fingers are *en fuego*! We are brilliant, and no more eloquent words have ever been banged upon a keyboard!

Wrong. There's *nothing magical about writing*, but we tend to think there's something special about it. It's just like seeing patients, teaching a course, running a meeting, planning a project: there's nothing "magical" about that. But we always think there's something special about writing. Yes, writing is hard; but it's wrong thinking to believe that it's not like any other skill you can learn.

Believing in the myth of the muse is understandable because many of us have so much anxiety around our writing. So many of us fear that we're not good writers. We're intimidated by the great, prolific writers in our scientific fields—"I'll never be published in *Science* or *Nature*!" "I'm no stinkin' Nobel laureate!" We beat ourselves up for not being those genetic lottery winners who write in their sleep (or who write INSTEAD of sleeping). We may have a 24-hour, running ticker tape in our heads chock-full of self-loathing, self-berating, imposter syndrome-ing negativity: "Why can't I be like so-and-so, what is wrong with me, why can't I just do it? Why can't I figure out what to say? I don't know what the heck this all means! The grant application/paper is just going to be rejected anyway, why bother! Grrrrrr! I feel bloated. I wonder if there's any chocolate around here? Maybe I should clean out the microwave." Stop being such a jerk to yourself!

News flash: if you're in academia, scholarship is the coin of the realm, the currency of the trade. Academia is all about inquiry and discovery. But unless you publish it, you can inquire and discover all you want, but you will have no impact on your science. If you're going to stay in academia or anything close to academia, you have to wrap your head around the fact that writing is your job. That's right, *writing is your JOB! So do your job every day!* Many of us need to flip our thinking. In academia, faculty members may start to believe that writing is just something we do to pad our resumes/curriculum vitae to get promoted, something extra we do to earn recognition. So we may start to equate scholarship with shallow attempts at self-aggrandizement, calling attention to ourselves, patting ourselves on the back, or icing the cake. That's wrong thinking. This kind of wrong thinking is a perfect excuse for the clinician investigator who went into medicine to help people—to prevent, treat, and cure diseases and conditions. What better way to be even more self-sacrificing than to give up your *personal* writing to be able to spend MORE time consumed in the care of your patients! Faculty members already put themselves at the bottom of the barrel—you don't eat regularly, sleep regularly, or go to the bathroom regularly, so if you're not attending to your basic human needs, it's hard to convince yourself to write regularly!

We'll do everything else to help other people, and never help ourselves, and that's the wrong thinking about this. You have to wrap your head around the fact that writing is your job. You have to change your thinking from "writing is about me and my CV and getting promoted," to "writing is my *obligation*, and my *job* is to share my knowledge, my discoveries, and my innovations to diagnose, treat, and cure patients!" The only way you get "that" out is by disseminating it publicly. Hence, publication. You have to do your job. You have to write!

Recommendations/Suggestions

When you start thinking of writing as your job, not just something to beef up your ego, then you might get more religious about writing. But how do you get over this idea that there's this muse? That there's something magical or mysterious about writing? That writing is a gift or a talent that you weren't born with?

Practice it—schedule it

We do all this negative self-talk, but writing is no different from anything else you do. Any other habit you acquired, you got there by what? How did you get to be good at taking a patient history, teaching a class or a group of residents, or running a lab? Practice, practice, practice. Like anything you're trying to learn—piano, performing a surgical procedure, another language, a new sport, you have to practice doing it.

How do you get over this idea that there's a muse? You write. You write regularly. How do you write regularly? You make it a habit. How do you make something a habit? You just schedule it in your calendar and do it. You can talk all you want about learning how to play the guitar. But unless you find a teacher, get a guitar, book the lessons, go to the lessons, and then practice, it's not going to happen! Similarly, you can talk all you want about all the papers you're going to write someday, but unless you schedule those writing appointments with yourself, meet yourself at those scheduled writing appointments, and do it, it's not going to happen.

Once you decide you *want* to do something, you commit to it. And then it becomes sacred and inviolable—it's *your* time. After all, you're the captain of your own destiny. No one's going to take more of an interest in your own career than you.

The best way that you're going to get better at writing is just by practicing writing. Don't wait until you "feel" motivated to write, just do it. And guess what? You're going to fail. Like practicing the piano, you're going to hit the wrong note and it's going to sound horrible. You're going to make mistakes. You'll set too high of expectations for your writing sessions. "I'm going to write for six hours, and during that time I'm going to finish that article, dissertation, and grant application and start those other articles." Ridiculous! That's too long a writing session, and it's too much work.

But through a WAG, you'll get really good at figuring out what can be accomplished during a certain time period. "Hm. It looks like I have 20 minutes between meetings today. Instead of going to Starbucks for a latte, I'm going to copy my odds ratios and 95 percent confidence intervals into table 3." "Yes, I see that I have a free morning, but I know I can't write text for four solid hours, so I'm going to outline a discussion section for 40 minutes, and then for 20 minutes, I'm going to read that e-alert table of contents from my journal to see if I need to download any of the articles. I'll take a 5-minute restroom break, check emails for 15 minutes (timed), and then for 45 minutes I'm going to run some regression models . . . etc."

After a while, that muscle memory of habitually writing becomes like hitting the right notes, or getting yourself in the front door at the gym, Weight Watchers, or Alcoholics Anonymous—it's no big deal! Writing will become just another of your habits. It will just be what you do— just your job! And you will be amazed at how unemotional (boring maybe?) your writing will become, because you're not freaking out about it anymore. Paul Silva (2007) says it like this: "If you allot four hours a week for writing, you will be surprised at how much you will write. By *surprised*, I mean *astonished*; and by *astonished*, I mean *dumbfounded and incoherent.*"

Automaticity—establish a routine

The concept of "automaticity in regimen" is a phenomenon of something becoming mechanical and automatic. When you do something so routinely, like brushing your teeth, it becomes mechanical and often mindless. You don't really think about it. In fact, it becomes so automatic that you sometimes wonder if you did it! Have you ever been driving your car and ended up at work when you intended to go to the grocery store? Or think about your morning routine. There's never been a day when I got in the shower in the morning and said, "All right. What's going to happen in here today?" I just get in and get out. Sometimes, I'm so "mindless" that I'll wonder, did I already condition my hair? Our morning ritual is a good example of how many of us are on auto-pilot during our morning routines.

We become accustomed to performing certain activities without really thinking about them. We kind of "zone out." You want your writing to be like that. Not that you're zoned out completely, but that your writing is not an angst-ridden, emotionally-laden, stressful experience of: "Am I going to write today? What am I going to write about? How am I going to say it?" No, you want it to be an in-out, automatic process.

When something becomes automatic or mechanical, it likely has little emotion attached to it. Automaticity in writing is great because we know that there can be a lot of emotion around writing. So if you just start writing routinely; for example, "I write every Monday, Wednesday, and Friday morning for 20 minutes before I even check my emails," you no longer wonder if you're going to get any writing done today, and you no longer beat yourself up at the end of the day for not getting any writing done, because it automatically happened. "Yes, of course I wrote today; I write every day! And, yes, I always condition my hair after I shampoo, so it's done . . . and I'm done!"

Make your writing times one of your ritualistic habits. When you do so, you will no longer freak out about it because it's something that's just natural. So if one of your writing myths or barriers is that you think there's something special or magical about writing, just schedule it! Make it ordinary, just part of your regular routine. Years ago, Dunkin Donuts had a television commercial with a guy shuffling up at 4:00 a.m., mumbling, "Time to make the donuts." That's just what he did—made the donuts. When your calendar or clock alerts you that it's time to write—go make your donuts.

Start on time and stop on time

As you're scheduling your writing time and getting into your routine, it is important to adhere to your start and stop times. Why do you think it's important to get in and get out on time? Well, the importance of starting on time is more obvious. You start on time because you respect yourself and you respect your time as if you're the boss. You would never show up late to a meeting with your dean or president. And once you finally show up to the meeting, you certainly wouldn't casually plop down with your Starbucks coffee, phone in your hand, skimming through emails, news, or posts. So don't be so casual about your writing time. Honor it, respect it. Treat yourself like a VIP. Show up on time, prepared to write. (We'll talk more about your preparation later; hint = agendas.)

But why is it important also to stop on time? If Laura's Outlook calendar says she's writing today from 2:00 to 3:00 p.m. and it's 2:50 p.m. and she's "in the zone," she may feel tempted to keep pushing over her scheduled stop time. Why should Laura stop at 3:00? She should stop for at least two reasons. First, if the conversation in her head is something like: "I can't stop now! I'm on fire! My brain is fully alive and I have fingers of fury! I'm channeling my genius!" Laura is falling prey to the myth of the muse. She's now in that "writing is mystical and magical" headspace. She may be afraid that if she stops when she's supposed to, she may never get "it" back. That is wrong thinking. You have to have the calm confidence that you *will* be back, probably tomorrow, and you'll pick right up where you left off.

The second problem with not stopping when you've scheduled to stop is that you are treading in the dangerous territory of *unplanned binge writing*. Emphasis is on "unplanned." Binging—on anything—is bad. We typically think of binge eating, which is obviously bad, but there are also folks who binge on what they consider benign or even good things. We binge-watch Netflix, binge-shop, and binge-exercise or binge-diet. Aside from being unhealthy and perhaps dangerous, the problem with a binge is that you cannot sustain it. If you ran a marathon yesterday and your running group asks if you're coming to the noon-time run, you may blast them with a: "Uh, no! Dudes, I ran the marathon yesterday! Duh. I need to rest!" You might be able to starve yourself for a day or two, but at some point, you will find your face in food—lots of it. What happens if Laura goes on an unplanned binge today and turns that one hour of scheduled writing into four hours? How will she feel right afterward? Yes, she'll probably have an immense feeling of accomplishment and satisfaction. But what happens tomorrow?

The conversation in Laura's head may sound something like this, "What's on my calendar today? I was to write from 11:00 a.m. to 11:30 a.m. But I wrote four hours yesterday! I deserve a break!" Wrong thinking.

Most of us cannot sustain regular writing binges because we do not have days with big chunks of hours set aside for our writing. What is achievable—and sustainable—is writing with increased regularity for shorter durations. Writing is your job. You do your job every day.

Earlier, I emphasized *unplanned* in binge writing. In academia, we know that sometimes those RFPs (request for proposals) or LOIs (letters of intent) are issued with very short turnarounds. On those occasions, you're engaging in full-out, game-on, *planned binge writing!* You certainly could not get by in that environment by saying, "Well, that RFP due in two weeks sounds right up our alley, but I'm in this WAG thing and I've committed to writing for 20 minutes a day. So we'll see what I can get done on the RFP in 20 minutes a day of writing." Nope. You're clearing your schedule, missing sleep, and writing your pants off.

But for the most part, you do not want to engage in *unplanned* binge writing because you may get into a bad habit of giving yourself an excuse to skip writing for a while.

Have a daily writing agenda

Previously, I talked about showing up on time for your scheduled writing sessions. I also mentioned the importance of coming prepared to write. Preparation involves planning! You could simply use your Outlook calendar function (or a notebook, spreadsheet, or Word document) to set your writing appointments, including very specific writing "agenda" items; for example, "Copy means and standard deviations from statistical output to table 1," or "Draft Introduction section." or "Fill in methods section," or "Assemble references." Your calendar appointment should *not* say, "Write," or "Work on grant," or "Finish dissertation." This is the difference between setting big, hairy, audacious goals and SMART (specific, measurable, achievable, relevant, and time-bound) objectives.

If you're a high *J* (judging) on the Myers-Briggs Type Indicator, you appreciate the value of making checklists, schedules, agendas, and itineraries, so you will naturally cozy up to this recommendation. If you're on the opposite of the dichotomy—a *P* (perceiving), you're more predisposed to spontaneity, flexibility, open-ended changeability, and less structure, so this will be more of a challenge for you. Try it anyway. See if having a little bit of structure helps you make progress. I don't know what else to suggest for you adorably spontaneous *P*'s; I'm an off-the-chart *J* compulsive planning list-maker who enjoys adding things I've already *done* to my *to-do* list, just so that I get the satisfaction of seeing it crossed off!

Summary:

- There is no writing muse.

- There is nothing magical or mysterious about writing; it is a skill that can be learned.

- Writing is my job. I will do my job every day.

- Schedule your daily writing; that which is scheduled, gets done.

- Routinize your writing; make it automatic like your morning ritual.

- Respect your writing appointment; start on time, stop on time.

- Avoid unplanned binge-writing sessions.

- Have a very specific writing agenda. Your calendar appointment should not say, "This is my writing time."

Three things I will START doing:

_____

_____

_____

_____

_____

_____

Three things I will STOP doing:

_____

_____

_____

_____

_____

_____

Three things I will CONTINUE doing:

_____

_____

_____

_____

_____

_____

CHAPTER TWO
The Myth of No Time

The second barrier to writing productivity is that there's no time. No kidding? Of course there's no time! There's no time for anyone. We're all running around as proud, card-carrying members of the "Cult of Busy." It's like we're hyper-stimulation addicts. "You think you're busy? Oh, that's nothing. I'm way busier than you. I haven't slept in three days, haven't eaten in a week, and I can't remember the last time I went to the bathroom." I had a former boss who during our weekly meetings would whine, "I haven't peed all day!" I suggested we hold future meetings in the restroom! We're all busy. Make a decision to slow down. In the immortal words of our generation's famous philosopher Oprah Winfrey, "If you don't want to burn out, stop living like you're on fire."

We all make time for the things that are important to us. We're all living and breathing and bumbling around our worlds. We're all fed, bathed, and clothed—at least periodically. You are managing to do a lot of things. Make writing one of those things! I know, it seems impossible to fit in one more thing, but you have to figure out what's important to you. If writing's important to you, make time for it. Learn to say no to things in your life that are not mission-centric, and learn to delegate some responsibilities, where appropriate. The tasks you delegate may not be your version of perfect, but they will probably be good enough.

How do you make time if you're a busy clinical investigator charting until 1:00 a.m. every morning? Or if you don't even control your own work schedule? Well, is there anyone else in your sphere who has managed to produce scholarship? How do they do it? Buy them a cup of coffee and ask them, "How in the world do you fit in your writing?" By the way, in a WAG, you will meet colleagues who have figured "it" out; you'll learn a lot from each other. Your lack of time may be another opportunity to flip your thinking script. A lot of people think they need big chunks of time to write. So if they don't have a whole day, a half day, or a two-hour chunk of time, they think, "Why bother writing? I don't have enough time to get into it!" Here's a newsflash: You're NEVER going to get a big chunk of undisturbed writing time. Ever. Maybe if you have the great (and rare) fortune of taking a sabbatical.

You don't have chunks-o-time to write, but you certainly have 10-, 15- , 20-minute windows here or there. I bet you do. Where? Well, instead of sitting in your early-morning traffic commute, could you stay home and write for 20 minutes until the peak traffic clears? Can you discipline yourself to check emails only during certain times of day and use other spare time to do a writing activity?

There is a time for everything, and a season for every activity under the heavens (Ecclesiastes 3:1).

My pastor said something recently that blew my mind—he was preaching on Ecclesiastes—King Solomon—the intersection of happiness and wisdom. Guess what he said. "The busier you are, the lazier you are!"

What the what? My head almost exploded from twisting my face up so much. His point was that it's actually much easier to just keep doing "stuff" and much harder to take the time to prioritize. We have to learn to say NO. Or say, "No, not now." It's all about setting appropriate boundaries. So the next time you think you or others are being so efficient because you're so busy, flip that upside down and think about those people who do NOT profess to be super busy, and look at their productivity.

We know that in our hyper-busy work cultures, there are people who manage to write. In fact, there are people who manage to publish a lot. In academic medicine, our rule of thumb is you should be publishing about three peer-reviewed manuscripts per year. People do it, so the easiest thing is to go meet the people who do it and ask them to share their writing habits. A WAG is a good first step to regain control over your time and writing goals.

Recommendations/Suggestions

Less is more. Get comfortable with brief writing segments.

This myth of having no time may also result because many of us think we need big chunks of time. We think we need a whole day: all Friday, all Sunday afternoon, or four whole hours to get into it. Wrong. You need less time than you think. This is also where you need to expand your definition of writing. You don't need big blocks of time to do small writing tasks.

If you only have 10 minutes, you can certainly copy and paste those means and standard deviations from your statistical output to a table. If you only have five minutes, you can skim through those abstracts from the email of your journal's most recent table of contents for reference material. Think of it as little writing workout bursts—like HIIT (high-intensity interval training)! You can go really hard for a few minutes and then get back to operating on patients, charting in Epic, meeting with your lab, etc.

If you stay in academic medicine, you will likely never get big blocks of quiet writing time. Never. So don't think of your writing as all or nothing. Reframe your scholarly writing as little snippets, every day.

There are a lot of things that have to happen to get a paper published. You have to "project manage" your papers. Think of that paper as a product on an assembly line. What are all the things that need to happen to get it out the door? If you were to go on a "mythical" sabbatical and were writing instructions for someone else to write those papers, what would those instructions look like? You would be very detailed, leaving no room for error. And there would probably be hundreds of steps. Each of those piecemeal steps would take a certain amount of time; you will become very good at estimating time to complete those steps. Furthermore, project managing your paper will also point out some of your glaring paper-writing-process inefficiencies and downright deficiencies.

Retrain your brain into operating via those SMART (specific, measurable, achievable, realistic, time-constrained) objectives, and you will learn that you don't need those big chunks-o-time.

Stop multi-tasking!

Time is fleeting, compressed, and very precious. As such, we think we need to multi-task. Naturally, we all think we're great multi-taskers. We're like an octopus—balancing the desktop, the laptop, the iPad, the cell phone, the pager, the protein bar, etc. Everything's going on at once, and we think we're super good at it. News flash! You are not good at multi-tasking.

Actually, you suck at multi-tasking. If you don't believe that, ask the person in the car behind you when you're at a stoplight transfixed by your phone.

Keeping an eye on email is probably the worst multi-tasking habit we have. We all think that a quick look-see will help us stay on top of things. But of course, "looking at email" inevitably sucks us into the email time-space continuum, and then there go 30 minutes! It's downright Pavlovian how we've all trained ourselves to respond to the pinging, dinging, buzzing, and vibrating tones of our email alerts. So we're emailing, texting, working on a document, charting, answering questions from colleagues, thinking about eating or going to the restroom, etc. Multi-tasking costs you time and money; don't do it! There are empirical data showing that multi-tasking kills your focus. Task-switching can cost as much as 40 percent of your productive time (APA, 2017; Rogers & Monsell, 1995).

Writing is YOUR time. It's your WOD (writing of the day). Go at your writing WOD with a single-minded, focused discipline. Do nothing else during your writing WOD. Don't multi-task. Be in the moment. When you're writing, write. Do nothing else. Respect that time.

Be accountable!

One of the great things about WAGs is the accountability component. When you're in a WAG, you are forced to think about and publicly articulate your writing goals. Then you practice the writing behaviors and can make adjustments to your goals and/or your behaviors.

If Alicia says, "I'm going to write for an hour," and then—because she's aware of being accountable—she realizes that at the 40-minute mark she's mentally assembling her grocery list, she might then recalibrate her next writing session. She would simply schedule her next writing session for 40 minutes, and she'll be more focused and use her time more efficiently. Similarly, if Panagis commits to writing for half an hour in the morning before he leaves for work, but notices that he's taking that time to catch up on some sleep, he might try to move that half hour of writing to the evening after the kids are in bed. Or Jin may find that her 30 minutes of mid-day writing is ideal, but the location is bad because people know she's in her office and they can't help but interrupt her. Jin can practice training people how to treat her; for example, by putting the "do not disturb" note on her door and then honoring it by refusing to answer the door during that time. Or Jin can find another writing place in a small conference room, a colleague's office, a coffee shop, her car, a coat closet, etc.

So be honest, and hold yourself to the same standards you expect (or wish) of others.

Schedule your priorities

Schedule your priorities, don't prioritize your schedule. The former is proactive; the latter is reactive. If you're a person who has time-management problems, you schedule your priorities—that which gets scheduled gets done! You don't want to get into the habit of opening your calendar on Sunday night and lamenting, "What's going to happen to me this week? Apparently neither eating nor sleeping is what's going to happen to me this week!" No. To the best of your ability, you need to schedule time in your monthly, weekly, daily calendar to attend to your basic human needs and to your basic academic needs—thinking, innovating, writing!

You need to schedule your priorities because otherwise, those things that are important to you are less likely to get done if they're not on your calendar. In his 2×2 time-management matrix, Franklin Covey showed us how things are either urgent or not urgent, important or not important. Many of us spend too much time in the two bottom quadrants—things that are urgent and not important comprise the *Quadrant of Deception*. These are things like interruptions, some calls, some emails, some meetings, and some committees. The other bottom quadrant is the *Quadrant of Waste*; for example, junk email, social media, busywork, time wasters, etc. We need to work on avoiding these quadrants.

Naturally, we must spend time in the urgent and important quadrant, the *Quadrant of Necessity*. These are the true crises, emergencies, patient care issues, deadlines, teaching courses, running programs, etc. We need to learn to manage these tasks. However, the vital quadrant for your long-term success and leadership is where we should spend some time focusing on the things that are important, but NOT urgent—the *Quadrant of Quality and Personal Leadership*. For example, these activities include your career planning and preparation, focus on personal mission and values, relationship and team building, self-care, etc. Our career development, getting promoted, and serving in leadership roles is important, but that typically doesn't have the same time urgency of our innumerable job responsibilities, so we tend to defer those activities. We think: "No one is going to die if I don't finish writing that paper today. I can do it tomorrow." The problem is that tomorrow never comes.

Perform a "time and motion" study on yourself

If you feel like you have no time, really look at where you are spending your time. Ask one of your engineer or project manager friends to help you troubleshoot your process. Think about it as if you're doing a Total Quality Management or Continuous Quality Improvement project for patient safety and patients kept getting infections. You have to figure out, "Where is it happening? Where in the process is this happening?" You would follow a patient from the time they enter your hospital to the time they leave or if they return back to your hospital. You would observe all the points of contact to discover the weak link in your patient safety process.

The same way with you. If day after day, week after week, month after month you're not achieving your goals, do a quality-control study and observe your writing process. What happens when you walk in the door every day? What are your points of contact? Where do things fall apart for you? So it might be a time of day, a place, a person(s), a practice, a project, etc. that is your infectious zone or agent. That is where you're infecting yourself with this bad habit.

Your bad habit infection may start with your lack of organization. You may notice that you spent about 20 minutes looking for that darn document. Your prescription is to design a more organized file folder system. A brief TED Talk, workshop, or a cup of coffee with an uber-organized friend may be worth your time and effort if it results in your downstream writing efficiencies. Similarly, maybe you notice that your one-hour meetings could be shortened to 20 minutes or cancelled altogether. Maybe you notice that you have unwittingly trained your clinic staff or research lab staff to interrupt you with minor details.

Maybe your schedule for a certain period of time is particularly conducive to your performing certain writing tasks more readily than at other times. For instance, if you're on service for six weeks, you may schedule your writing activities to be focused on the more mechanical aspects of paper writing, such as working on tables, figures, charts, and writing up the results. When you're off service, you may schedule your time to focus on the more cerebral components of paper writing, like the introduction and discussion sections.

Or if your children have certain activities during the week that make Mondays impossible, then don't torture yourself by scheduling intense writing on Mondays. If you're a morning person, schedule your writing in the morning. If you're a night owl, do it at night. Work your schedule; don't let your schedule work you!

There is ample opportunity for all of us to improve our processes. A WAG is a good environment for you to practice your organization and learn from fellow WAGGERs.

Expand your definition of writing

You don't need four hours to write. You need less time than you think. WAGs are all about establishing a sustainable writing habit—by writing with more frequency and for less duration. It's easier to think about writing more regularly and for shorter periods when you expand your definition of writing. Think about writing as not only words, words, words, sentences, sentences, paragraphs and paragraphs, and pages and pages. I suggest that writing is any activity we do that results in another line being put on our CV or biosketch.

How do we get another line on our CV/biosketch? It isn't just text. It's designing the study, collecting the data, coding the data, cleaning the data, analyzing the data, and creating tables, figures, charts, and graphs. It's writing the letter to the editor or the response to the reviewers. It's all the email correspondence with co-authors. All of that stuff comprises the business of writing.

So now that you recognize all those discrete activities as part of your writing practice, you might see how little chunks of time are amenable to certain writing activities. If you don't have adequate time or blood in your brain to think clearly, you can certainly zip through the journal's email displaying the next issue's table of contents and determine if you need to download an article for later reading or referencing. That only takes 5 minutes! As the operating room is turning over, you can certainly copy means and standard deviations from the SAS output into table 1. In between patient consults, because you have a scribe who is doing your epic notes for you and you've taken to wearing an adult diaper since you never have time to visit the restroom, you can dictate a couple "implications for the field" sentences to yourself to include in the discussion section of your paper. Or you can go to your Outlook calendar and assign yourself some writing tasks for later. Think about it. What writing activities can you accomplish in 5–10 minutes?

Summary:

- Escape from the "Cult of Busy."

- The busier you are, the lazier you are. Learn to say no.

- Take back control over your schedule. Avoid the tyranny of the urgent, and the conspiracy of interruption.

- You need less time than you think. Start with 10-minute writing snippets.

- Project manage your work. Think piecemeal.

- Stop multitasking; it kills your focus.

- Be accountable—to yourself and your fellow WAGGERs.

- Schedule your priorities; don't prioritize your schedule.

- Expand your definition of writing. The writing enterprise doesn't solely consist of text, text, text.

Three things I will START doing:

_____

_____

_____

_____

_____

_____

Three things I will STOP doing:

_____

_____

_____

_____

_____

_____

Three things I will CONTINUE doing:

_____

_____

_____

_____

_____

_____

CHAPTER THREE
The Myth That You Don't Know How to Start

The third myth is that you don't know how to start. You may be at a complete loss as to how to even begin writing a paper! Do I start at the very beginning? That means I need a clever, catchy title. So that means I cannot do *anything* until I nail a title, right? Wrong. Scholarly writing is not a linear process.

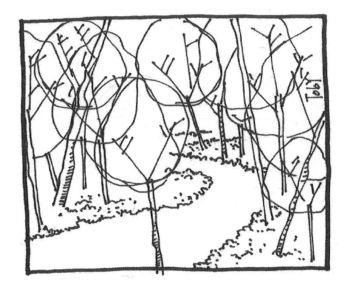

My paper-development process tends to look like this: methods, introduction, results (text and tables/figures), introduction redux, discussion, abstract, title. You can always start with the methods because you know what you did or what you plan to do. While you're waiting for the results, start writing your introduction and jot down some notes for what you will say in the discussion.

Some of us have trouble starting because it all seems too big a task. It's why some people can't even conceive of getting in shape, because it seems like too much—it's an entire lifestyle edit including eating differently, drinking differently, changing routines, maybe changing friends, joining a gym, exercising, and tracking calories eaten, calories burned, miles run, etc.! By the time you think of all the things you have to do to get in shape, or publish that paper, you're exhausted!

Some of us think we don't know how to start writing a paper because we really don't *know* what we should write about. Or we think, "Who will care about *that?*" Certainly you've read lots of other people's papers and have an idea about the big, medium, or small things they write about. Aren't you sometimes surprised by the things people write about? Believe me, there's an audience for everything! Think about your projects. Sometimes you don't need to wait until a project is done to write it up. You can always write a literature review; you likely already have a pretty good handle on the literature in your area if you've started a project! Or you can write up your methods, a how-to or "how we did it." Or an editorial, commentary, or early findings report.

Some of us have trouble starting a new paper because we fixate on the parts we hate. You may get yourself all worked up because you're dreading writing the introduction section or the discussion section. Or maybe you don't know how to best illustrate your results. Or maybe English isn't your native language and you struggle to write at all. This is where we tend to let our emotions control our behavior. We dread doing things we suck at, right?

If you're an off-the-chart introvert, you likely dread the thought of having to socialize at a huge party! If you're a big-picture thinker, you'll dread the meetings involving lots of spreadsheets and financial reports. If you're a hard-core, rational, logical thinker, you might feel homicidal if you are put on a work team with sensitive, emotional, feeling types. If you're a regimented planner, you'll dread working with a procrastinating, spontaneous teammate.

So it just makes sense that your paper-starting paralysis may be the result of innate preferences for certain activities and corresponding innate non-preferences for other activities. But that does not mean that you cannot *learn* and become *competent* in the things that don't come naturally to you. We learn by practicing. In a WAG, you will at least practice a writing activity for 30 minutes a week. In a WAG, you will also practice being accountable to yourself and others for setting and achieving concrete daily and weekly writing goals.

And don't fall for that "writer's block" nonsense. Paul Silvia (2007) writes: "Writer's block is nothing more than the behavior of not writing. Saying that you can't write because of writer's block is merely saying that you can't write because you aren't writing . . . The cure for writer's block is writing."

The accountability you practice in a WAG heightens your awareness of how you use your time. If you, perhaps aided by the observation of your fellow WAGGERs, identify a pattern of behavior that is sabotaging your productivity, you can then troubleshoot. You can *learn* a new skill, by taking a course in biomedical and scientific writing, survey methods, structural equation modeling, Excel graphics, etc. Or you can *learn* to turf the parts of writing you hate to your co-authors or trainees!

Recommendations/Suggestions

Think SMART (specific, measurable, achievable, realistic, time-constrained)

Instead of thinking of your writing in terms of BHAGs—big, hairy, audacious goals—reframe your thinking into SMART writing objectives. Don't think: "I have to write that paper. I have to finish that grant." That's a BHAG, and that's nasty. Instead, think: "I will bullet-point list my discussion section. I will talk with X about my three specific aims." The former list is simply overwhelming; the latter list is an easy checklist.

It's like a person waking up in the morning and finding a sticky note on the fridge that says, "Lose 50 pounds. Win lottery. Find a cure for all cancer." The person's like, "What the what? That was today?"

They're running down the hallway, vaulting back into bed, and securing the covers tightly over their head. "Nope, not today, not gonna happen . . . !"

But many of us do just that to ourselves. We come into our office every day and the sticky note on the monitor says, "Finish those two old papers and start and finish those next three papers." Then at the end of every day, we walk to the car, bus, or train with our superhero capes dragging on the ground, and in our best *Winnie the Pooh*'s Eeyore voices, we say, "Oh bother. Just another day I didn't finish those two papers. I just knew I wasn't going to start those other three papers. Woe is me." All these dejected superheroes beating ourselves up, muddying up our capes, believing that we suck.

But if that person wakes up in the morning and the sticky note on the fridge says, "Eat a salad and drink a bottle of water. Join Match.com. Post a peace sign on Facebook." Now, the person says, "Hm. Well, that certainly seems doable. I can probably manage all that today."

Similarly, if we come into our office and the sticky note says: "Copy Odds Ratios and 95 percent confidence intervals from output to table 2; read through e-alert table of contents from the journal; and email co-author to remind her about deadline"—you're in a very different ballgame, my dear. Because now you can rip that sticky note off the monitor at the end of the day, crumble it up, and mic-drop it! Mission accomplished! At the end of that day, your superhero cape is blowing in the wind and you feel invincible. So long, Eeyore! It's really empowering when you have accomplished the daily tasks you set for yourself.

Think recipe or template

If you're new to academic writing, try a template. Get a model of a good paper that resonated with you: you liked the style, the readability, the use of tables, the discussion section, whatever! Or get some paper written by the top guns in your field!

I literally did that in graduate school. I printed out papers of my favorite author (thank you, Dr. Frederic Wolinsky), and I would mimic his style in terms of laying out the argument, presenting certain types of tables, talking about the data in a specific order, etc. I unabashedly copied his style, and told him so at a professional conference.

If your goal is to publish in a specific journal, ask your mentors or colleagues to send you the Word versions of their papers most recently published in that journal! That way, you can simply gut their scientific text, but you have the layout, the headers, sub-headers, abstract format, etc. without killing yourself going through those hideous Instructions to Authors. That can save you hours.

If you like a colleague's tables, graphics, figures, or charts, ask for the template! It's much easier to plug and play your own data into Excel than to try to remember how to get those stupid 95 percent confidence interval brackets to fit each separate bar.

Or simply open up your last published paper and re-save it as a new file under a different name (using Save As under the File tab in Word). This new file will be the starting point for your new paper. Certainly do NOT plagiarize even your own self, but save yourself some time and effort with your ready-to-go cover page, contact author information, references, and tables. It's much easier to edit and change a document than to start anew.

The point is, every project need not start from the ground. You don't have to build a new mountain every time you write a paper. Give yourself a head start by using template language or writing recipes.

Delegate

You don't have to be the expert at everything. As a famous gazelle-like model wife of a well-known quarterback (who shall remain nameless because he's not my team's quarterback) once lamented after a bad loss, "My husband can't THROW the ball AND CATCH the ball!" I know this example might feel like a bit of a stretch, because in academia, most of us have been trained to indeed both THROW and CATCH everything related to our scholarship. However, the most published investigators I know are on teams of co-authors. I can only name a handful of academic investigators who have done a lot of publishing alone.

So kiss your ego goodbye and have a "come-to-Jesus" meeting with your friends and co-authors: "I have made an important lifestyle decision. I will never again open up a statistical analysis program, nor will I ever attempt to try to recreate those individualized 95 percent confidence interval bars in Excel. I hereby anoint you as my statistician, and you as my bar-tender. I shall bask in the glory of reading the literature and writing the manuscripts." Or something like that. This requires that you, first of all, get some co-authors. Ideally, you assemble a paper-writing team machine that includes someone who loves designing studies, analyzing data, writing, editing, doing graphics, crafting letters, uploading manuscripts for submission, etc. Then you just get out of each other's way, hold each other accountable, and get those papers out the door!

Robotize your work

Another way of thinking about your scholarly work is like an automated, assembly-line product. When manufacturing a snow shovel, there are engineers who conceive of the shovel design, and engineers who design the molds that will make the shovel components. The various shovel components can be produced at different times and places and assembled at a later time.

Similarly, you and your team (think co-authors) may conceive a product that happens to be a patient safety intervention. You might then bring in other team members (think study design experts, statisticians, database managers) from the hospital to help you design the process "mold" for how that intervention works. Based on the information your hospital-based team provides, your "shovel" design may be modified (think edits). Then your intervention machine starts producing the patient safety "parts" (think manuscript sections) and you assemble those parts for a final intervention product (think finished manuscript).

So, if you think about your papers as manufactured products, you can robotize your work. You could not tell your Amazon Alexa to "write my paper, finish my grant, do the IRB." Alexa, in her eye-rolling, polite, and annoying voice, would reply: "I'm sorry, I do not understand. Try again, dummy." Rather, if you told Alexa to "Re-run the last ANOVA model after adding an interaction term of education and income," you're getting somewhere specific.

Try putting very specific "to-do" tasks on your writing agenda; for example, draft the first two introduction paragraphs; insert a 5×4 table and label the rows and columns; copy means and standard deviations from output to table 2; brainstorm five possible titles; email co-author *X* and ask for three sentences about future implications, etc.

An added value to this kind of thinking is that your time management and organization skills will likely improve. When you project-manage your work, you can't help but get good at knowing how long a specific task actually takes. If you've never done something yourself, you have little to no appreciation for the effort that task involves. For example, it's one thing to *assign* your program coordinator the task of organizing an annual project review meeting. Many people have absolutely no idea how difficult and incredibly time-consuming it is to organize a single meeting, let alone a big event. But if you've done it yourself, you have a pretty good sense of all the moving pieces and parts and how long it should take; e.g., typically two to three times longer than anyone thinks. Similarly, when you start paying close attention to all the discrete elements of your writing projects, you will get a really good idea about how much time you *actually* spend doing certain activities compared to how much time you *wish* you spent doing certain activities.

You may think you only spend about 20 hours mucking around in your data, but when you really look at your workflow, you'll see that it's more like 80 hours because you forgot about all the data management that precedes your analysis. Reviewing literature can also be a huge time suck. It's very easy to fall down the rabbit hole of reading *all* the literature because each manuscript inevitably leads you down all their references. Upon reflection of your "manuscript production company," you may identify where your bottleneck(s) lie, and then you can make process improvements.

Summary:

- Yes, you know how to start! Start writing what you already know: the methods, some references, a blank table, your name on the title page!

- Don't perseverate about the parts you hate.

- Think SMART objectives vs. big, hairy, audacious goals.

- Use a writing recipe or a template.

- Delegate. It's not efficient to be the expert at everything.

- Think like a robot. Assign yourself very specific writing tasks.

Three things I will START doing:

_____

_____

_____

_____

_____

_____

Three things I will STOP doing:

_____

_____

_____

_____

_____

_____

Three things I will CONTINUE doing:

_____

_____

_____

_____

_____

_____

CHAPTER FOUR

The Myth That You're Not Ready to Start

Some of you may be thinking: "I don't have trouble starting. I know how to start writing! I'm just not READY to start writing!" That's the fourth myth—that you're just not ready. Of course you're not ready, because, naturally, you need to read 550 more journal articles, or run 45 more regression models, or have six more co-author meetings, or recruit 100 more patients or samples, etc. So clearly, you're not ready to start writing! But as soon as you get those things done, you'll be ready.

We can all come up with several dozen really good reasons why we're not ready to start writing. It's easy to procrastinate starting something, especially when it feels arduous. New Year's revolutionaries are an obvious example. Some of us decide that on New Year's, or for Lent, or starting Monday, I'm going to diet, start exercising, stop drinking, learn to knit, etc. Paul Silvia (2007) talked about how professors yearn for three-day weekends, spring breaks, and the summer months, only to return to work grumbling about how little they wrote: "The first week after summer break is a din of lamentation and self-reproach." How do you get around this pattern of self-flagellation? Just do it already! Or in Silvia's words, "Write the damn thing." Don't wait . . . for anything . . . to just *start* writing.

If not procrastination, maybe you've just given up on starting altogether? In her book *No Sweat*, Michelle Segar talks about the problem of giving up on things. She explains that we tend to give up on things that result from *negative motivations* for *unpleasant activities* that have *no immediate gratification*. She uses exercise as an example, but scholarly writing fits just as well! She says the first step is to reframe the activity as a gift to yourself, something that you want to do, something that is rewarding. Then, you should try to make the activity pleasurable, because pleasurable things are sustainable. Try flipping your thinking about writing, from something you *have* to do to something you *want* to do. Then, focus on the part of your writing that you enjoy doing.

Many of us think we're not ready because we feel like we don't know what we're going to say. "How can I start writing when I don't know what I'm going to say?" You're not quite sure how to tell a convincing story, how to interpret the data, how to make sense of your findings in light of what other people have reported, how to discern the important points in the context of your study's limitations. It can be overwhelming.

Here's the thing: writing is not what you do *after* you've figured it out; writing is *how* you figure it out. What? Sure, there are probably a few people out there who get ideas in their sleep and they wake up with a "Eureka! I've just figured it out!" But most of us mere insomniac mortals are not the recipients of such divine inspiration. Instead, we have to hammer away at it, slog through it, and just tough it out. We have to "write it out to figure it out."

When I was a young kid, I took piano lessons from Sister Mary Williams back at the Villa Maria Elementary convent in Erie, PA. When Sister Mary Williams would give me a new piece of sheet music after my lesson, what do you think I would do with it when I got home? Would I sit at the kitchen table night after night with my Oreo cookies and milk and study the new music piece? No, of course not. I would go right to the piano and I would play it out. It would be awful at first, but I would keep practicing it until I got it right. It's the same for writing—you sit at that keyboard and you play it out until you figure it out!

So again, try reframing your thinking. Yes, you are ready to start writing. Right . . . now! You don't have to wait until it's all perfect in your head. Just start writing something.

Recommendations/Suggestions

Start writing as soon as you have the idea

You don't need to wait until your "project baby" (your paper) is born and graduating high school before you "tell the family" (publish) about your little bundle of joy. Think about journaling the life of that project baby from conception! Try creating a file folder called "Scathingly Brilliant Ideas." Under that file folder, you could have several documents of your "starter" papers. Every time a new project or paper comes to mind, start writing it! Why not? Paul Silvia (2007) says, "Your first drafts should sound like they were hastily translated from Icelandic by a non-native speaker . . . Let the id unleash a discursive screed, and then let the superego evaluate it for correctness and appropriateness" later!

Maybe you've just left an interesting seminar about a new data analytic methodology and you wonder if you could apply the same methods to your data. Sketch it out! What would it look like? Draft a title, bullet-point some introductory statements about why this is important and what it adds to the field, recall what you learned in the seminar and note what you will do in your methods section, then put in some placeholder figures showing what you might expect your data to show. Jot down some phrases for your discussion section answering the "so what?" question. That document may sit there for a while or it may never even be born, but the seed may grow into another project, and in the meantime, you've had the mental and physical practice of writing it up.

Write it out to figure it out

Remember, writing is *how* we figure things out, not what we do *after* we've figured things out. Silvia (2007) says, "Writing breeds good ideas for writing." You don't need to wait until you have all of the details before you start writing; you're more ready than you think. Once you start writing, you will notice the missing elements in your paper and you can simply make a note on one of your writing agendas to follow up and fill in the gaps later.

Don't convince yourself that you have nothing of import to say. Many of us in academia tend to underestimate the value of our work. You may think that until you have a Hope Diamond (45.52 carats), there's no point in presenting your little half-carat diamond. Write up your literature review, a how-to on assembling your trans-disciplinary research/clinical team, your methods procedure, and/or your early results.

Expand your definition of writing (redux)

Sometimes we feel like we're not ready to start writing because it feels like *having* to run a marathon without having done any training, and you just know it's going to hurt and you're going to quit. But don't think that way. Remember to expand your definition of writing. Think of little writing chunks. You don't need to run the whole marathon today; how about you just jog on over to the corner? Little bite-sized writing sessions are much more palatable AND sustainable.

Remember, writing is any activity that is associated with the end product that ultimately gets put on your CV or your biosketch. Your scholarly writing does not consist solely of words, sentences, paragraphs, and pages of text. We know that our scholarly writing also involves: designing the study; collecting the data; cleaning and coding the data; analyzing the data; assembling and formatting references; assembling footnotes, tables, figures, charts, and graphs; writing letters to the editor and reviewers, and reading literature.

So if you hate writing the discussion section and you're in a nasty mood, don't do it! Do something else; just do something! Describe the methods; that's the easiest thing because you're just describing what the heck you did.

So, when we expand our definition of writing, the 10 minutes between meetings becomes a period of time that can be used for a very specific writing activity—like outlining a section of the paper or sketching out a causal model on a scrap of paper.

Delegate!

News flash: you don't need to be the expert in all things! As academicians, many of us have reached a high level of success because we had to demonstrate excellence in lots of things. God forbid we ever asked anyone for help with anything. Wrong—so incredibly inefficient! You have a team. Get smarter about working with your colleagues and co-authors. This is especially tough for perfectionists, but if someone in your inner circle can "do the job" 80 percent as well as you can, let 'em have at it, and let it go!

Delegating work is both liberating and terrifying, especially if you're a control freak. But try it. Each of us is trained and gifted in one or more areas, and each of us struggles in one or more areas. Why not identify the unique talents that lie within your team members and allow them the opportunity to shine doing what they love? If someone on your team makes killer slides or graphics, you should never waste a moment in PowerPoint or any kind of graphics illustration program. If you have a data manager or statistician, you had better not be coding data and analyzing data. If you have a communications major on your team, they're writing or heavily editing your introduction and discussion sections. You get the idea. A surgeon doesn't perform a procedure all alone. Every person in that operating room has a vital job to perform. Think of your paper as that patient on the table. There are a lot of people who have been trained to do a very specific function on that paper; let them do their job. Don't let that paper die on the table because you were running around the room trying to do a dozen other jobs.

Summary:

- Yes, you're ready to start—right now!

- Don't wait *until* anything! There are pieces that are dying to be written right now.

- Writing is not what you do *after* you figure it out; writing is *how* you figure it out!

- Write as soon as you have the idea.

- Expand your definition of writing; think of small writing activities you can accomplish in bite-sized chunks.

- Delegate. Get your team started on their writing parts now!

Three things I will START doing:

_____

_____

_____

_____

_____

_____

Three things I will STOP doing:

_____

_____

_____

_____

_____

_____

Three things I will CONTINUE doing:

_____

_____

_____

_____

_____

_____

CHAPTER FIVE

The Myth That You Don't Know How to Finish

The final myth is that you don't know how to finish. Many of us in academia are here because we're perfectionists. And the trouble with perfectionism is that nothing is ever good enough! Which is the kiss of death for generating scholarship. Remember, the currency of the trade, the coin of the realm in academia, is peer-reviewed publications—so you must get those papers out the door! Don't let your perfectionism thwart your progress.

You've heard the saying, "Perfect is the enemy of good enough." Take that literally; your paper is likely good enough! It will never be perfect, and if you insist on perfection, you will take forever to amass those coins of the realm. In fact, Silvia (2007) says: "Perfectionism is paralyzing."

My buddy, Dr. Dave Yousem, a world-renowned neuroradiologist here at Hopkins, and I give a pretty regular talk called: "Get that Paper Out the Door!" He always handles the *perfectionism* segment, and on each and every slide, he has a typographical error. It drives me nuts. But he does it on purpose to convey the idea that the talk was still good, even though it wasn't perfect. I love the quote he uses by Michael J. Fox: "I am careful not to confuse excellence with perfection. Excellence, I can reach for, perfection is God's business." Dave's three basic concepts have to do with identifying a publishable unit (he uses the analogy of a 10 carat white diamond vs. 20 single-carat diamonds), determining if you are at a publishable moment, and whether your paper is "editorable."

Dave leads a public confessional where we all admit to the age of some of our paper "babies." "How many of you have been working on a paper for more than nine months, a year, two years, three years, etc.?" We all have those trouble kids. If you're one of those people who has toddler-aged papers, you have trouble finishing. It is reasonable that we end up working on a paper for upward of a year. It may even creep into two years by the time we've seen it through revisions and resubmissions to the same, or different, journals. But if you're still gestating a three- to five-year-old paper(s), there's a problem.

Take inventory of your papers. How old are they? What are your *excuses* for harboring those fugitive papers? You just need to do another literature search and read a few more articles? You just need a few more samples, patients, or data points? You just need the statistician to run a few more analyses? You need your co-authors to do something(s)?

At some point, you just have to be brave and put yourself out there. What's the worst that could happen? Will the League of Scientific Writers swarm your institution and revoke your degrees? Now, of course I'm not advocating for your submitting a pile-o-poo, but your manuscript will never be perfect, so just submit it and see what happens! You have to realize that (probably) never in the history of science has an author received the following from a journal editor:

Dear Author,

Thank you for your brilliant manuscript on this most enlightening and timely topic. It is absolutely perfect and we plan on publishing it in our next issue. Keep them coming!

Love,
The Journal

Even the best-written journal articles will require some editing. Knowing that, submit it and give the reviewers some job security! Believe me, if you've missed referencing THE seminal piece of literature in your field, don't you think they'll tell you? If you've transposed a figure or misinterpreted something, aren't you pretty confident that the experts in your field will catch it (assuming your co-authors don't have your back)? What's the worst-case scenario? They're not going to call your dean and say, "This one here, you better look at his credentials. We have some serious concerns about his legitimacy." Of course not.

Entrust someone from your inner circle, maybe a fellow WAGGER, to read the paper and help you with any needed tweaks or adjustments. Just don't be fixated on things being perfect. Don't wait and wait and spin and spin and spin. You're losing your time. You're losing your window of having an impact. You may even run the risk of being scooped, especially if you gave the paper at a conference and somebody heard you (which happened to me)!

Recommendations/Suggestions

Triage

Learn to triage your work. Triaging refers to sorting patients/victims in order of medical necessity or priority. For example, you would treat an apparent stroke in higher order than a dislocated shoulder. Similarly, think of your papers that are *thisclose* to done as "the stroke"—get that guy in the operating room! It's all hands on deck to save that paper and get it out the door. Don't let those *thisclose* papers languish while you're noodling around with a new paper idea or filling in tables of data on some other paper.

I oftentimes use the example of an industrial stove cooktop in a restaurant when I'm talking with my WAGGERs. In a busy restaurant kitchen, there are many food orders in various stages of preparation and readiness. Think of those food orders as all your projects (because if you're fortunate, you don't *only* have one project at a time). Every burner on your stove is filled with something because you are involved in many projects. At any point in time, you have to be smart about triaging those projects in order of importance. The simmering sauce on the back burner may be moved up to the front when the journal responds with a "revise and resubmit within two weeks," and correspondingly, that rolling boil of water may have to be moved to the back burner and turned down for a minute while you attend to the sauce. You're constantly moving pots and pans around the kitchen, and that's what you do with your papers. You should not doggedly pursue one paper from beginning to end at the expense of other papers. You have to become adept at switching gears and managing your projects.

Recalibrate your level of effort

This suggestion has to do with the perfectionist's insistence on making *everything* perfect; hence, bringing their *A* game to each and every activity. If you really want to increase your efficiency, learn when to bring your *A* game, your *B* game, and your *C* game. I know. Some of you may need a moment here . . . Take a deep breath and humor me. If you are obsessive-compulsive about everything you do, you are working way harder than you need to work. Clearly, we *must* bring our *A* games to our "urgent and important" job tasks, like patients, students, and leaders' assignments. Of course you're going to do your best work as you prepare to present your research at your national conference. However, if your local church, synagogue, or temple asks you to give a presentation to their congregation, you should *not* be preparing for that talk at the same intensity as your professional conference. Ideally, you're pulling out a recent talk you gave on the topic, brushing it up a bit, and moving on. That's your *B* or *C* game.

It would be a huge misallocation of time for you to treat all your projects and papers as if each required the same level of effort. If you're spending the same amount of time writing letters of recommendation for your trainees as you spend writing grant applications, something's wrong with your system. Your time is precious and incredibly valuable, so don't waste it spending disproportionate time on things that give little return. WAGs will help keep you accountable to your effort.

Ration your time

This suggestion may work if you suspect (or know) that you are spending an inordinate amount of time doing a particular task. For example, if you like doing data analysis, it is probably very easy for you to spend dozens of hours playing in your data. When you are in your comfort zone, you can literally lose track of time and zone out running various regression models. Or if you like to read, you could spend several weeks simply reviewing the literature.

However, we know that spending too much time on something means we're likely avoiding something else. So ration the time you spend on your various writing components. This requires that you keep track of the time you *actually* spend on a task, and compare it to the time you *budgeted* for that task. Think of yourself as one of those drug-sniffing dogs; find that time, follow that time, and don't lose that time trail! Good dog!

You might start rationing your time by simply allotting an estimated number of minutes or hours to perform a certain activity; for example, literature review: 10 hours; study design: 40 hours; data collection: 100 hours; methods section: 4 hours; data analysis: 80 hours; results section: 2 hours; discussion section: 20 hours; introduction section: 10 hours; abstract: 2 hours. Then, keep track of how much time you actually spent on those activities, and that will be your new "formula" to use for subsequent writing projects.

On your next project, you'll apply that same formula and see how closely it aligns. You'll likely find that some activities move more quickly or slowly. For instance, for a series of papers in the same project, you likely won't have to spend much time reviewing the literature; you'll merely scan for anything new that has been published. But at least with some specified time parameters, you're forcing yourself to justify the extra time on something. Do I really have to spend 8 more hours analyzing the data, or do I already have the answers to my research questions/hypotheses?

A WAG will help you ration your time by being accountable. In a WAG, you're forced to publicly state your writing goals for that particular timed, communal writing session, as well as your goals for the following week. As you practice that goal-setting and goal-achieving/goal-failing skill, you will be more keenly aware of your use of time.

As you become more aware of the time required to achieve certain goals, your overall project management skills will improve. You will then find that you have the ability to more accurately calculate what can be done, when, and how.

Don't obsess about things being perfect. Get that paper out the door! Let the reviewers chew it up. Get it back, fix it, and get it back out the door ASAP!

Summary:

- Don't let perfectionism thwart your progress; get that paper out the door!

- Learn to triage your projects and papers; academic writing is not a linear process.

- You don't need to bring your A game to every single thing in your life.

- Become a time tracker; dog your time and don't lose it.

Three things I will START doing:

_____

_____

_____

_____

_____

_____

_____

Three things I will STOP doing:

_____

_____

_____

_____

_____

_____

Three things I will CONTINUE doing:

_____

_____

_____

_____

_____

_____

CHAPTER SIX
WAGs (Writing Accountability Groups)

<u>How-to</u>

WAGs meet one hour a week for 10 weeks. The hour session is broken up into a 15-minute segment, a 30-minute segment, and then a final 15-minute segment. WAGs are peer-facilitated groups; that is, no mentor-mentee, supervisor-supervisee dyads or other "bosses" in a WAG—they can start their own WAG! WAGs need to be a safe place to talk about writing barriers, fears and anxieties, hiccups in writing goals, and other career issues.

<u>How do I start a WAG?</u>

You can get your own WAG started by simply sending an email (see Appendix for template email) to friends, colleagues, people in your group, division, or department, wherever. You only need four to eight people, including yourself. Once you have the people, send out a poll to identify the ideal meeting day and time. Once you've established the day and time, identify the meeting location. It's best if you stick to the same location for your ten-week WAG.

WAG prep work: 10 days and then 1 day before your first WAG

Ten days before your first WAG, resend your original WAG email invitation reminding folks about the WAG—the day, time, and location. Strongly urge everyone to show up on time, because after all, they would *never* show up late to a meeting with the dean, would they? Of course not. So WAGGERs treat themselves with the same dignity and respect. They show up on time to ALL of their WAG sessions and other scheduled writing appointments with themselves! You should also send the brief WAG pre-assessment tool (see Appendix) which measures frequency of writing and duration of writing sessions.

WAG day 0—orientation day

At your first meeting, you should do introductions (name, title, department, research interest, or other relevant information) and have everyone state the 10-week writing goal(s) that they indicated in their WAG pre-assessment. You should then review the WAG rules and process. The WAG rules are as follows: one hour a week for 10 weeks; WAGGERs should attend all sessions, must be on-time, and must agree to be accountable. The WAG process is: 15-30-15.

- 15 minutes of goal reporting from the prior seven days (not applicable on the first day) and goal setting for today's 30-minute writing segment

- 30 minutes of writing

- 15 minutes of goal report-out and goal setting for the next seven days

Who will be our WAG facilitator?

You should then decide on who will be the peer facilitator—it will likely be you. Peer facilitators keep the time and keep track of the WAGGERs' goals. Peer facilitators can hold the job for the 10-week WAG or can rotate the role between the other WAGGERs. Peer facilitators may have to be the "crack-the-whip" timekeepers and goal trackers. Remember that the key concept in WAGs is accountability. So each WAGGER has to be accountable to the group and to themselves—WAGGERs must commit to attending most, if not all, of the 10 WAG sessions before they even start a WAG. WAGGERs must also commit to getting to the WAG on time and adhering to the WAG process. One suggestion is to start your WAG 10 minutes after the hour as opposed to an on-the-hour start, because people never seem to be able to calculate transportation time between meetings!

So pretend that this is your WAG and this place is your WAG meeting space. This is how the WAG will work. It's Monday and you and your fellow WAGGERs (minimally four WAGGERs, eight WAGGERs maximum) are going to meet here in this room for the first time.

Alicia says, "Okay, everybody. I'm glad we could all make it on time! As a reminder, we've all committed to meeting here in this room for 10 Mondays in a row from 11:10 a.m. to 12:10 p.m. Starting at 10 minutes after the hour ensures that we can all physically get here on time. Let's start with introductions. Everyone, please state your name, department, research area, and 10-week writing goal(s)."

If you all know each other and your research areas, you may proceed directly to the 10-week writing goals. Your peer facilitator, in this case Alicia, will be summarizing each WAGGER's 10-week writing goal(s) in a spreadsheet, or notebook, or Word document (see Appendix for a sample goal spreadsheet). After everyone has had a turn, Alicia will review the weekly WAG process: 15 minutes of goal reporting and goal setting, 30 minutes of "writing," and 15 minutes of goal reporting and goal setting.

Here at Hopkins, I kick off every new WAG by going to the first day and talking about writing myths and barriers and how the WAG works. I also bring a copy of Paul Silvia's book *How to Write a Lot* for every WAGGER. (Now I guess I can also give them my WAG Your Work book). So maybe this is where you hand out books to your fellow WAGGERs and jump into a discussion around common writing myths and barriers:

- The myth of the muse

- The myth of no time

- The myth that you don't know how to start

- The myth that you're not ready to start

- The myth that you don't know how to finish

WAGGERs will chime in with their own personal barriers, and you will then talk about some strategies and WAG recommendations that are in this book and in the WAG materials (www.WAGYourWork.com).

"We are what we repeatedly do. Excellence, then, is not an act, but a habit." — *Aristotle*

WAGs are not about the *content* of your writing; that is, there is no editing or review of each other's writing. You can learn writing skills and/or editing skills somewhere else. WAGs are all about the *process* of writing—building good, sustainable writing habits. This is accomplished through a weekly writing WAG session minimally, but ideally via increased regularity of writing (e.g., daily or a couple times a week) and decreased duration of writing sessions (e.g., 10, 20, 40 minutes).

What happens during the 30-minute timed communal writing portion?

WAGGERs expand their definition of writing. That is, during the timed communal 30-minute writing period, all WAGGERs will not necessarily be typing words on their laptops. An expanded definition of writing means that any activity that is part of the scholarly process is considered writing. Think of writing as any activity that results in your adding another line on your curriculum vitae, resume, or biosketch. For example, reading literature; collecting, coding, and analyzing data; making tables, figures, charts, and graphs; assembling references, writing letters to the editor and responses to the reviewers, etc., all count as writing.

So, after this orientation day, everyone should be motivated to begin WAGGING! Everyone should briefly state how much and when they intend to write during the next seven days until you WAG again. Send a thank-you email and a WAG reminder!

WAG day 1

This is it! Alicia welcomes and applauds everyone for being on time.

The first 15 minutes is spent going around the room and reviewing the goals—accountability—the goals you set last week, and then talking about what your goal is for today's writing session. It might go something like this:

Alicia: "OK, everybody, let's go. It's time. I'm looking at the spreadsheet.

Jin, last week you said you were going to write three times a week, Monday, Wednesday, and Friday, for an hour. How did that go for you?"

Jin: "Great. Monday/Wednesday I crushed it. Friday my friends came in from Washington, DC and we went out for dinner, so I took a half day off, so I kind of blew it on Friday."

Alicia: "That's no problem. What are you going to do during today's timed writing session?"

Jin: "I want to review some literature for my paper. I have a couple of emails from my target journal. I'm going to read through the abstracts and see if I need to download, read, and include any of the articles."

Alicia: "Great. Michelle, last week you told us you were going to write five days a week for half an hour. How did that work out for you?"

Michelle: "Nailed it. Monday, Tuesday, Wednesday, Thursday, and Friday I wrote for 30 minutes just like I said, and in fact, I tacked on an extra 15 minutes on Tuesday/Thursday because my meetings were re-scheduled, so I got a little extra time."

Alicia: "Wow, great! What are you going to do during today's timed writing session?"

Michelle: "Well, today during the half-hour session my goal is to copy the means and standard deviations from the statistical output into table 2 of my paper and then clean up the table."

Alicia: "Sounds good. Panagis, I see in the spreadsheet that last week you said you were going to write for an hour on Monday and Friday."

Panagis: "Yep, I did it. No problem."

Alicia: "What are you going to do today?"

Panagis: "Today I need to work on my references, so I'm uploading some references into my reference manager."

Alicia: "Great. Last week, I told you all that I was going to write three days a week—Tuesday and Wednesday for 40 minutes and Friday for 20 minutes, and I did. I also snuck in an hour on Saturday morning. Today I want to draft my discussion section, especially the first two paragraphs."

That discussion happens in the first 15 minutes. As the WAGGERs get to know each other better and the group gels, members will not only feel comfortable encouraging each other, but they will also feel more comfortable holding each other *accountable* via tough love. For example, WAGGER *A* says to *B*: "Three weeks in a row now you said you planned on doing X and you never quite did X. You might want to rethink that. Have you thought about trying . . ." Or "Who are you kidding, Panagis? We know you're not a morning person. Why do you always say that you're going to write in the morning and then you get so disappointed in yourself when you didn't write in the morning? Why don't you think about shifting your writing to the end of the day?" Undoubtedly, WAGGERs will say, "I found this great app a friend of mine told me about that tracks your writing," or "You guys need to see this new website I found . . ."

WAGGERs will start to recognize their own and others' patterns of good and maladaptive writing behaviors. This heightened awareness via accountability helps to identify process improvement opportunities! And of course, your WAG will organically grow into a small community of engagement—a social support network!

Academic medicine is a very competitive, isolating environment. You need people who have your back. Part of having your back is holding you accountable. During that first 15 minutes, the discussion centers on holding yourself and each other accountable to the writing goals you articulated in the prior week and provides an opportunity for stating and then accomplishing today's writing goal. You'll also find yourselves offering moral support, encouragement, and peer-to-peer life coaching!

The WAG 30 minutes

Then Alicia will say, "OK, friends, our 15 minutes is up. It's time for us to write." The next 30 minutes is that timed communal writing session where everybody's doing their thing. As you noticed from the examples I gave earlier about "expanding your definition of writing," that activity can look very different for each individual WAGGER.

So Alicia sets a 30-minute timer and you're off! Someone may be reading literature, someone may be working on figure 2, someone is copying statistical output to table 1, and someone is drafting their discussion section. You're all doing something different. It doesn't take too many of these 30-minute sessions for WAGGERs to develop a keen sense of what they can and cannot reasonably achieve in that time period.

WAGGERs also learn to appreciate what can and cannot be done by observing how their fellow WAGGERs use that time. If you're stuck in the mindset that "writing" actually means you have to be tapping away at a keyboard hammering out words, sentences, paragraphs, and pages, now you broaden your scope of the writing enterprise as including data management and analysis; creating tables, figures, and charts; organizing references, drafting letters to the editor/reviewers, and even reading or researching.

It's up to you to determine your peak text-writing, data analyzing, literature reviewing, and table-making times and rhythms. Maybe you find that your WAG time is best for writing manuscript or grant text, or maybe you find that you accomplish more during your WAG time when you focus on reviewing the literature. Part of the WAG process is identifying your writing process strengths and weaknesses, which has a lot to do with your current work-life obligations and personal preferences. If your WAG meets at 6:00 p.m. and you're a morning person, you'll probably feel good working on your most cognitively-challenging writing task. However, if you're a morning person and your WAG meets at 3:40 p.m., you might only have the energy to copy means and standard deviations from your statistical output to table 2. Discerning your writing habit efficiencies and inefficiencies is a WAG byproduct.

The last 15 WAG minutes

Then Alicia says, "The 30 minutes is up! How did we do?" Again, here starts the *accountability*. Did you do what you said you were going to do during this 30-minute communal writing session? And, "What's your writing plan for the next seven days until we WAG again?"

Alicia: "Jin, did you do the first paragraph?"

Jin: "Yep! It's not perfect, but I feel pretty good about it."

Alicia: "What do you intend to do for the next seven days until next week's WAG, Jin?"

Jin: "Well, I'm going to check out that app and I'm going to write for half an hour Monday, Tuesday, Wednesday, Thursday, and Friday."

Alicia: "Awesome, great!"

Alicia: "Nancy, did you read through the literature list?"

Nancy: "Yes, I did. In fact, I found a good article that I need to incorporate into my manuscript."

Alicia: "Great. What are you going to do for the next seven days until our next WAG?"

Nancy: "Unfortunately, I'm travelling to New Guinea for that conference, but on the airplane I'm going to spend some time thinking about and just free-writing on this new paper."

Alicia: "Sounds like a great use of some 'protected' time!"

Michelle: "I am really motivated. The statistician just sent me some other stuff. During the next seven days until I meet you all, I'm going to write from two to four on Monday, Wednesday, and Friday. Tuesday/Thursday I'm going to write in the morning for half an hour."

You get the idea . . . as the peer facilitator, you simply go around the table at the start of the 30-minute session and ask each WAGGER to state whether or not they accomplished what they set out to accomplish.

Again, WAGs are focused on accountability with the end goal of helping you to establish a sustainable writing habit. Think of a WAG like Weight Watchers, Alcoholics Anonymous, a fitness boot camp, a marathon training routine, musical instrument lessons, a personal coaching session, etc.; you have to articulate a goal or goals! For example, you want to lose X pounds, avoid alcohol, increase muscle mass, run a marathon, learn to play guitar, or be a better leader. WAGs will help you establish a regular writing routine that will work for you.

When we document and publicly state an intention, we are more accountable to it and hence more likely to accomplish that intention. Part of the reason the WAG process works is because no one wants to be "that guy"—the one who either doesn't show up or doesn't do what she or he says he or she's going to do! There's something about a deadline that kicks many of us into gear. So if you see the WAG on your calendar and you haven't done "it," chances are you're going to double down and get 'er done! Then, magically, this accountability to your fellow WAGGERs and accomplishing your writing goals becomes a new self-fulfilling prophecy—"I said I was going to do X, and by gosh and by golly, I did X!—YEEHAW!" Your confidence will go through the roof!

Summary:

WAGs are like CrossFit or a boot camp for writing. It's the workout of the day, which just happens to be writing! Ideally you want to write daily, even if only for 10-20 minutes. Your goal is to increase the frequency of your writing and shorten the duration of each session. That's the whole goal of WAGs: accountability and getting you into a habit.

How do you get into a habit? Ideally by writing more regularly in shorter durations. Why? Because you can sustain that throughout the life of an academic career or even a business career. No matter what your life is like now, it's only going to get busier. If you're going into academia or currently in academia, especially academic medicine, you will likely NEVER have the luxury of a regular chunk of hours, let alone a whole day, of uninterrupted writing time. What you can sustain is writing for 10, 20, or 30 minutes every day or almost every day. Undoubtedly, if you haven't already drunk the Kool-Aid, you will be ushered into the "Cult of Busy" where it's a badge of honor to out-busy the next person. So make sure you schedule your writing into your crazy busy schedule.

So, let's recap. How can you sustain a regular flow of scholarly contributions (peer-reviewed publications, grant applications, reports) or your personal writing projects (books, articles, blogs)? By writing in small snippets. That's the whole point of a WAG: getting you into the habit of writing routinely by learning accountability in a small group. And how will it work? You're going to WAG every week for an hour, for 10 weeks. You'll do 15 minutes of reporting out from the past seven days and goal setting for the communal writing session. Then you'll do your 30 minutes of communal writing. Then you'll finish with your reporting out and goal setting for the next seven days. You'll end up building a small community of engagement where you'll make new friends, colleagues, and potential collaborators. You'll hold each other accountable, give each other constructive feedback, and support and encourage each member to achieve their goals. You may notice a sort of "social contagion" around writing, such that everyone in your WAG will become infected with the WAGGING virus!

At the end of your 10-week WAG, you will find (via the brief post-assessment—see Appendix) that WAGGERs will report writing with greater frequency and for shorter durations. You will also likely note satisfaction with new writing habits, a greater sense of control over the writing process, improved time management, and confidence for a future of scholarly productivity. You may also find group enthusiasm to schedule another 10-week WAG!

CHAPTER SEVEN
Discussion

The greatest good you can do for another is not just to share your riches, but to reveal to him his own.

—*Benjamin Disraeli*

My hope is that you will joyfully discover one of your riches in a WAG. As I stated previously, the goal of a WAG is to establish a sustainable writing *habit* by writing with increased regularity and for shorter durations. For a 10-week period, you will meet once a week for an hour with at least three other people (a total of four to eight WAGGERs). During your weekly WAG, you will start with 15 minutes of updating each other on the writing goals you set last week and if you did or did not accomplish those goals, and then you'll also state your 30-minute writing goal for that WAG session. Then you'll all engage in your 30-minute writing activity. Then you'll spend the final 15 minutes reporting whether or not you accomplished your stated 30-minute writing goal and also what your writing goal(s) is for the next seven days until your next WAG.

Remember that the key concept in your WAG is accountability. I know I'm being redundant here, but I need to remind you of a few things. Everyone should show up on time to the WAG. To facilitate an on-time start, try starting your WAG at 10 minutes after the hour to allow transit time (e.g., 11:10 a.m. or 1:40 p.m. vs. 11:00 a.m. or 1:30 p.m.). Make sure your WAG peer facilitator is someone who is a strict taskmaster; i.e., the one who is always mindful of the agenda, the time, and keeping on task. Your WAG peer facilitator should NOT be the one in your group who always loses the WAG spreadsheet, is always late, and can't stay on topic. Follow the 15-30-15 agenda.

I'll leave you with some WAG mantras:

- Writing is my job. I will do my job every day.

- Write or write not. There is no *try*.

- There is nothing magical or mysterious about writing; writing is a skill and I can learn it.

- I am not a binge writer.

- I schedule my priorities; I don't prioritize my schedule.

- I write as soon as I have an idea.

- I have expanded my definition of writing.

- I robotize my work.

So, why not WAG? What do you have to lose? Once you get into your weekly WAG and start scheduling daily or almost daily writing, you might also discover the value of scheduling and prioritizing other important things in your life—like joy, fun, family, and friends! A WAG will help you control the writing beast, lest it control you. You will schedule your writing so that your writing won't schedule you. And then you will have created guiltless space in your life for joy. After all, as Silvia (2007) wrote: "Is academic writing more important than spending time with your family and friends, petting the dog, and drinking coffee? A dog unpetted is a sad dog; a cup of coffee forsaken is caffeine lost forever."

Academia is tough, medicine is complicated, and writing is hard. So you've chosen tough, complicated, and hard to earn your living. But the good news is that there are thousands of other masochists out there who also want to make a difference in the world by doing tough, complicated, hard things. When all is said and done, "We're just all walking each other home" (Ram Das), so let's just WAG a little while we walk each other home.

FAQs

Why 4–8 WAGGERs?

WAGs are *limited to four to eight people (WAGGERs)*. Why? If you have anything fewer than four people, when two of you are out of town at a conference, on service, or on vacation, you have a WAG of one or two, and all of a sudden, you're no longer a group. Anything more than eight and it's too difficult and unwieldy to manage everyone's schedules; it's like trying to get all the puppies in a box or herding cats. So, four to eight participants ends up being a nice size WAG.

Why 10 weeks?

Why is a WAG 10 weeks and not five or 12 weeks? First of all, WAGs are scheduled in 10-week blocks to provide a "hard start-hard stop" book-end to your work. During each 10-week WAG, you will set very specific writing goal/goals, and it is best to have a finite period in which to accomplish that goal. That way, you're creating a time-bound sense of urgency. Otherwise, if you simply schedule a WAG for every Wednesday at noon, you might be tempted to skip various WAG sessions, because in your mind, "I have every Wednesday for the rest of my life to WAG; it's no problem if I skip *this* Wednesday!" You will find that scheduling a 10-week WAG block will help you grow in your confidence around establishing and achieving your writing goals.

During repeated WAG blocks, you will also get much better at project managing your scholarship. You will start to appreciate exactly how much time it takes you to complete all the writing components of a particular manuscript, grant application, or book simply by articulating and tracking your progress. Thus, on subsequent writing projects, you will be able to budget your writing time more efficiently.

Second, during each WAG session, you will be engaged in the "writing process" for 30 minutes. So, if you do no other writing during your workweek and the half hour at your WAG is the ONLY writing you do, at the end of your 10-week WAG, you will have written for five hours. Five hours over 10 weeks may be more time engaged in scholarship than many busy clinical investigators typically manage. And it also seems that five hours is a good amount of time to establish a habit.

In addition to the purely procedural benefits of a small group, there are other benefits to WAGGING in a small group. What naturally happens is that your WAG becomes a small *community*. These small WAG communities of engagement help minimize isolation, provide social support, improve collegiality and morale, and provide increased opportunities for networking and collaboration.

How do I start a WAG?

You can get your own WAG started by simply sending an email (see template email in Appendix) to friends, colleagues, people in your group, division, or department, wherever. You only need four to eight people, including yourself. Once you have the people, send out a poll to identify the ideal meeting day and time. Once you've established the day and time, identify the meeting location. It's best if you stick to the same location for your 10-week WAG.

Does reading your literature search count as writing?

Yes. Any activity that ultimately results in us putting another entry on our CVs or biosketch counts! Some folks in your WAG may be reading abstracts or articles, some may be entering data, some may be analyzing data, and others writing the letter to the journal reviewers, making charts or figures, or writing actual text.

What should I do during my WAG?

Do whatever works for you. Figure out what is most efficient for you during your weekly WAG time. Be accountable to yourself. It's personalized. Maybe you won't be able to do certain writing activities with others in the room, or maybe you'll discover the exact opposite—

that you're inspired by your fellow WAGGERs to do certain writing activities during your WAG. There is a social contagion aspect to doing a "thing" with others. Just figure out what your thing is and do it.

Am I the only one who is struggling with writing?

Nope. We are all in the same boat. We're all busy. We're all overwhelmed. We're all insecure about writing. Writing is hard. WAGs are a tool to help you develop a sustainable writing habit. Writing gets easier when it becomes a habit. And WAGs become vital support networks. You will undoubtedly build new friendships and maybe collaborative relationships. It's just human nature to bond with your fellow WAGGERs after you bare your writing-accountable soul week after week!

What happens after our 10-week WAG is over?

You renew your "WOWs" (and vows) for WAGs! Most WAGGERs end up re-WAGGING; i.e, signing up for another 10-week WAG jag. Stick with the 10-week WAG protocol, because it's good to set very specific writing goals for a discrete period of time. Otherwise, if you just say that you're going to WAG indefinitely, WAGGERs WILL stop coming because it's harder to justify skipping 1 of 10 sessions of something compared to skipping 1 of 52+ sessions of something.

You may bring on some new WAGGERs when you re-WAG, so don't set your newbie WAGs off on a bad foot. Keep to the 10-week schedule. Remember that 10 weeks is a good amount of time to set a habit. Because if you're not writing any other time, especially for busy clinicians in schools of medicine, at least you're writing for half an hour a week for 10 weeks. That's five hours of writing in a 10-week period.

Can someone join our WAG mid-stream?

No. It is not advisable to let someone join your small WAG community during a 10-week WAG period. They can join, if there's room (recall WAGs are limited to four to eight members), when your 10-week WAG ends. Why? Because you're building relationships with each other; you're creating a safe WAG place, you're establishing trust, and starting to feel safe talking about your writing barriers and challenges. Having someone new join your team mid-season may be awkward for the existent WAGGERs as well as for the newbie. Finish your 10-week session, ask who wants to re-WAG, and then determine if there's room to add someone new.

Can people remotely WAG?

For your first WAG, ideally, all members *should* be physically present. Why? Because people are more accountable when they're physically present. Conference calls are great examples of why you *shouldn't* support folks WAGGING remotely—because we all know what we do when we're on a conference call: we're checking and sending emails and sometimes barely paying attention to the call. When we WAG, we need to be focused on WAGGING—and nothing else. It's much easier to focus on your writing activity when you're in a room with other WAGGERs also trying to focus on their writing activity.

That said, seasoned WAGGERs do WAG remotely—synchronously and asynchronously. When they're traveling around the world or around the country. They'll Skype or Facetime into their WAG so they're synchronously writing. Or asynchronously they're checking in with their WAG (which might be 3:00 a.m. Kenya time) and reporting their progress on weekly writing goals, stating their intention for the weekly WAG writing session, the outcome of their sole writing sessions, and their seven-day writing goals. But again, I would only suggest you consider this alternative arrangement after your WAG has matured.

My team has decided to submit a grant application. Can we use a WAG to work on writing the grant application?

Sure! Remember, that the purpose of a WAG is to establish a sustainable writing habit by writing more regularly—with greater frequency—and for shorter writing session durations. Grant deadlines can be pretty quick, so when we see those juicy RFPs (requests for proposal) or LOIs (letters of intent), we're likely signing on for *planned binge writing!* Grant applications don't get done writing 20 minutes a day; you're usually spending intense writing hours during a brief period of time. Of course a WAG might be a good tool to get your co-investigators, lab, and team all writing their parts. If it's possible, given everyone's hectic schedules, using a *daily* WAG might just be the way to meet that grant deadline. Everyone is held accountable for writing or doing their portion of the application, and everyone commits to setting discrete daily writing goals.

Do WAGs fail?

Sure. The most common reason why a WAG fails is lack of participation. What happens is that someone organizes a WAG but doesn't get real buy-in from the participants. It only takes a couple WAGGERs to start skipping meetings here and there, until the whole WAG falls apart. It's like any group activity—happy hours, walking clubs, fitness teams, Bible study, volunteer groups—lost people equals lost motivation. Make sure all your fellow WAGGERs commit to the process. You don't want someone bringing donuts to your Weight Watchers meeting, and you don't want someone taking calls during your yoga practice. Similarly, don't invite someone to your WAG who will be sabotaging the group's efforts at being accountable toward establishing a sustainable writing habit!

Another reason why a WAG might fail for you is if you're overly ambitious. Remember, a WAG is 10 weeks. New WAGGERs tend to get super excited and rattle off a list of goals for the 10 weeks: "I'm going to submit paper A, start paper B, work on paper C, analyze data D, submit grant E, submit IRB protocol F, and start collecting data for grant G." That's just cuckoo's-nest craziness. But what's great about a WAG is that you will quickly learn how to appropriately scale your work and time.

After about three WAG sessions, you'll start calibrating your writing engine and get into a manageable rhythm. You'll start noticing the goals you achieve and the goals you avoid: "Hm, when I say I'm going to write in the morning at seven o'clock, I usually don't. Why? Well, I'm not a morning person and I hate to write in the morning." Duh. It's like your friends at the gym saying, "So, we'll see you tomorrow morning for our run?" If you're a night owl and you abhor getting out of bed before you absolutely have to, you're not going to want to run in the morning. And you're not going to want to run in the morning especially if you don't like to run. Don't be your own worst enemy. You'll figure it out—by being accountable to yourself and your fellow WAGGERs, you'll find your sweet spot.

What can we do to make sure our WAG is a success?

Start with a group of fellow WAGGERs (four to eight total) who are truly committed to the process. You want to be in a group of people who are sincere in their desire to establish a sustainable writing habit. They must understand what they're signing on for; that is, WAGGERs agree to meet once a week for 10 weeks, to follow the 15-30-15 rule (15 minutes of goal reporting and goal setting, 30 minutes of a writing activity during the communal writing session, and 15 minutes of goal reporting and goal setting), and to be accountable to yourselves and others. WAGGERs should show up on time, prepared! No multi-tasking allowed during that 30-minute communal writing session.

But don't take my word for it. Here's what WAGGER Matt wrote:

We tried to be really adherent to starting on time, recapping our goals from the previous week, what we hoped to achieve. At 15 minutes, we were starting... Usually about 2 minutes before the end of the 30 minutes, someone would give a heads-up, "You have 2 minutes to go!" That's when you'd start saving your work, sort of figuring out where you are, talk about it, set some goals. I think you're right, Kim. It's over those 10 weeks we got better at really identifying what were achievable goals. Instead of being like, "I'm going to write three hours a day seven days a week," and then coming back and being like, "Well, I actually only got in two days a week for a half hour," by the time you've done that two or three times, then you're kind of like, "Maybe my goal should be three times for a half hour, not seven times for 30 minutes."

Outside of my weekly WAG, how much writing should I be doing?

That all depends on you and what you can *realistically* achieve! Remember that you're trying to establish a *sustainable* writing habit. How can you incorporate a regular writing practice in your fluid work-life and home-life routines? If you're a busy clinician investigator, your calendar is probably nuts. When you're on service, you're probably praying for moments to be able to empty your bladder. However, what gets scheduled gets done! Can you schedule 10-minute writing snippets? That requires that you organize your writing "playlist," but once you have your organized list of specific writing tasks, you'll be able to maximize those brief writing times. Experiment with certain days of the week, times of day—mornings, afternoons, evenings—and notice what works best for you. Scheduling it and actually doing it may sound impossible, but it's like working out. Once you get yourself through the gym doors, you're good to go! So just get through that metaphorical writing door and do it.

Are there any motivational tricks for writing?

Starting or joining a WAG is the easiest "trick" because you just have to show up. WAGs follow a structured format, and you will see immediate writing results because if you do no other writing, at least you will be writing for 30 minutes a week for 10 weeks.

There are probably hundreds of recommendations for how to establish any habit, be it exercising, adopting a healthier diet, or learning a new skill, and they all probably involve *practice.*

So how do you motivate yourself to do something? Don't think about it, just do it. If you sit around and contemplate, "Should I go to the gym? I really should go to the gym. I haven't been to the gym in a week. I need to go. If I go now, I can be home by o-dark o'clock, or maybe I could just go tomorrow . . ." After all that conversation in your head, you might not go. So simply schedule your writing time and go! Don't even consider asking yourself the question, "Should I write today?" Look at your calendar, see your writing appointment, get to your appointment on time and prepared. Then just do it.

If you need a physical reminder, try it. Some people sleep in their gym clothes to avoid any excuses in the morning, or they place their gym shoes next to their bed, or they put their gym bag in the car with them so they're not tempted to go home after work (and then end up staying home). So if you need a special writing space, create one. If you need to wear a special writing cap, shirt, or bracelet to trigger you, do it. If you need to drink a special writing beverage or light a special writing candle, do it. Just do it.

How can you provide extra motivation for your WAG? Call yourselves something special, like one of our Hopkins WAGGERs—they call themselves the "WAGGING Wildcats." Another WAG set up "text support"; it's a play on *tech support*, where they will text each other if they need a boost! Or after a couple 10-week WAG sessions, have a "Renewing our WOWs for WAGs!" Remind yourselves all you've accomplished in your prior WAG(s), talk about what techniques and tools you've learned work for you, talk about ongoing challenges, and support each other. Have a little contest; anyone who doesn't meet their weekly WAG goals puts a little money in a pot that is used to buy a round at happy hour after the 10-week WAG.

My friend, colleague, mentor, and "big sister," Dr. Jennifer Haythornthwaite, is a professor of psychiatry and behavioral sciences here at Hopkins, and has been NIH-funded her entire career. In her Master Mentor program, she talks about motivation, and she challenges faculty members to do regular self-assessments. If we practice this kind of *internal accountability*, we can identify our vulnerabilities and devise strategies that play to our strengths and minimize our weaknesses. For example, she talks about *cognitive vulnerabilities* such as low self-efficacy ("I just can't write; it's impossible") or social comparisons ("I'll never have 500 publications like that Nobel laureate"). We need to practice realistic self-appraisal. You're right, most of us slightly-above-average-intelligence humans will NOT have 500 publications. However, we also need to remind ourselves that behind every thick curriculum vitae (CV) is the "anti-CV" showing all the rejected manuscripts and unscored grant applications—and that one is even fatter than the regular CV.

So stop comparing your insides to other people's outsides; you don't know their "innards." *Emotional vulnerabilities* have to do with performance anxiety ("What will my mentors think of me when they read this manuscript draft?"). *Behavioral vulnerabilities* have to do with time management problems ("I have too much on my plate right now; I don't have time to write") and avoidance ("I'll get to my writing this weekend . . . or maybe next weekend").

So, here you are. If you've come this far, you've poured yourself a big ole glass of the Kool-Aid, so go ahead and drink it! Hop on the WAG-ON. If you fall off, just take a deep breath and jump back on. I promise you, if you work the WAG, the WAG will work for you. The accountability will keep you focused. Achieving your daily and weekly writing goals will inspire you and give you newfound confidence for a successful career in academia.

Remain calm and WAG ON!

APPENDIX

Template Email to Start Your Own WAG

Howdy Friends! I've recently learned about WAGs (writing accountability groups).

A WAG is an active writing group that meets once a week over a 10-week block and follows a strict agenda of 15 minutes of updates and goal setting followed by 30 minutes of individual writing, and then 15 minutes of reporting and wrap-up. A WAG is limited to four to eight members, and you MUST commit to attending at least 8 of the 10 weekly sessions.

In a WAG, there is no peer review of our writing. WAGs are focused on the *process*, not the *content*, of writing. The goal for WAGGERs is to write with increased frequency and for shorter durations; i.e., to develop a sustainable habit of writing.

Check out the WAG webpage: www.WAGYourWork.com.

Are you interesting in WAGGING? If so, please reply to my email with several weekly days and hour slots that work for your schedule!

Writing Accountability Group (WAG): Pre-WAG Assessment

Author: Kimberly A. Skarupski, PhD, MPH

Associate Dean for Faculty Development

Office of Faculty Development

Johns Hopkins School of Medicine

Dear Fellow WAGGER: Thank you for making the commitment to join a WAG! For group accountability purposes, we will be collecting pre- and post-WAG data.

1. Please indicate your name:

   _____

2. How often do you write?

   a. Every day

   b. Almost every day

   c. Once a week

   d. Twice a month

   e. Once a month

   f. Rarely

   g. Never

3. How often do you wish you would write?

    a. Every day

    b. Almost every day

    c. Once a week

    d. Twice a month

    e. Once a month

    f. Rarely

    g. Never

4. What is the duration of your typical writing session?

    a. 0–15 minutes

    b. 16–30 minutes

    c. 31–45 minutes

    d. 46–60 minutes

    e. 1–2 hours

    f. 2+ hours

5. What duration do you wish you would write?

    a. 0–15 minutes

    b. 16–30 minutes

    c. 31–45 minutes

    d. 46–60 minutes

    e. 1–2 hours

    f. 2+ hours

6. Please check your barriers to writing.

____I have trouble getting started.

____My perfectionism prevents me from finishing.

____I have too many clinical commitments.

____I have too many teaching commitments.

____I have too many administrative commitments.

____I have too many personal/family commitments.

____I have difficulty with time management.

____I don't have adequate statistical/data analytic support.

____I don't have anyone (mentors) to give me feedback and encourage me.

____I am not very interested in my topic.

____I don't know what to write about.

____English is not my first language.

____My writing skills are poor.

____Other, please specify:

7. In the list above, please CIRCLE your biggest barrier.

8. Please specify your writing goal(s) for this 10-week WAG session:

9. Please specify your writing goal(s) for the next six months:

10. Please specify your writing goal(s) for the next year:

Thank you!

Writing Accountability Group (WAG): Post-WAG Assessment

Dear Fellow WAGGER: It's been 10 weeks already! Let's see how we did!

1. Please indicate your name:

   _____

2. How often do you write?

   a. Every day

   b. Almost every day

   c. Once a week

   d. Twice a month

   e. Once a month

   f. Rarely

   g. Never

3. How often do you wish you would write?

   a. Every day

   b. Almost every day

   c. Once a week

   d. Twice a month

   e. Once a month

   f. Rarely

   g. Never

4. What is the duration of your typical writing session?

    a. 0–15 minutes

    b. 16–30 minutes

    c. 31–45 minutes

    d. 46–60 minutes

    e. 1–2 hours

    f. 2+ hours

5. What duration do you wish you would write?

    a. 0–15 minutes

    b. 16–30 minutes

    c. 31–45 minutes

    d. 46–60 minutes

    e. 1–2 hours

    f. 2+ hours

6. Did you accomplish the writing goal(s) you established pre-WAG?

    a. Yes

    b. No

7. Please describe your WAG experience in terms of any new writing habits you have established. (E.g., are you satisfied with your WAG experience? do you feel like you will be able to sustain any new writing habits? Do you feel an improved sense of control over the writing process? Do you notice any improvement with time management? Do you feel as if your WAG has become a small community of engagement/social support?)

SAMPLE WAG GOALS TRACKER

THE WAGGING WILDCATS (Wednesdays, 12:10-1:10 p.m., 2nd floor conference room)						
	Alicia	Panagis	Michelle	Jin	Amir	Tomeka
WAG WEEK #1						
Attendance	present	present	present	present	present	present
7-day personal goal achieved?	n.a.	n.a.	n.a.	n.a.	n.a.	n.a.
WAG 30-minute communal writing goal	Table 1, draft intro.	read 3 articles, letter to editor	copy output to Table 3	outline discussion	make a bar chart	write up results
Goal achieved?	yes	yes	yes	yes	yes	mostly done
7-day personal writing goal	30 mins. daily	MWF 1 hour (20-mins. X 3)	TR 1.5 hours before bed	M-F 20 minutes after last patient	AM 30 mins; PM 30 mins.	M 1 hr, W 30 mins.

	Alicia	Panagis	Michelle	Jin	Amir	Tomeka
WAG WEEK #2						
Attendance	present	absent	present	present	present	present
7-day personal goal achieved?	yes		no	yes	mostly	yes
WAG 30-minute communal writing goal	Table 2, revise intro		copy output to Table 4	fill in discussion paragraphs	revise bar chart	start discussion
Goal achieved?	yes		yes	yes	yes	yes
7-day personal writing goal	40 mins. daily		TR 1.5 hours before bed	M-F 20 minutes after last patient	AM 40 mins; PM 40 mins.	M 1 hr, W 1hr

SAMPLE WAG GOALS TRACKER (continued)

THE WAGGING WILDCATS (Wednesdays, 12:10-1:10 p.m., 2nd floor conference room)						
	Alicia	Panagis	Michelle	Jin	Amir	Tomeka
WAG WEEK #3						
Attendance	present	present	present	absent	present	present
7-day personal goal achieved?	yes	yes	yes		yes	no
WAG 30-minute communal writing goal	outline discussion	upload paper	draft abstract		format references	revise intro
Goal achieved?	yes	no, almost done	yes		yes	yes
7-day personal writing goal	1 hr. daily	MWF 1 hour (20-mins. X 3)	TR 1.5 hours before bed		AM 40 mins; PM 40 mins.	M 1 hr, W 30 mins.

References

Allen, David. *Getting Things Done: The Art of Stress-Free Productivity*. 2001. Penguin.

American Psychological Association (APA). 2017. "Multitasking: Switching Costs." https://www.apa.org/research/action/multitask.aspx.

Boice, Robert. *Advice for New Faculty Members: Nihil Nimus*. 2000. 2014. Pearson. Random House Trade Paperbacks, New York, NY.

Duhigg, Charles. *The Power of Habit: Why We Do What We Do in Life and Business*. Amazon Digital Services.

Robbins, Mel. *The 5 Second Rule: Transforming Your Life, Work, and Confidence with Everyday Courage*. 2017. Mel Robbins Productions, Inc.

Rogers, R. D., & Monsell, S. (1995). "Costs of Predictable Switch Between Simple Cognitive Tasks." *Journal of Experimental Psychology*: General, 124, 207–231. doi:10.1037/0096-3445.124.2.207

Segar, Michelle. *No Sweat: How the Simple Science of Motivation Can Bring You a Lifetime of Fitness*. 2015. Amazon. http://a.co/5yEvp94.

Silvia, Paul J. *How to Write a Lot: A Practical Guide to Productive Academic Writing*. 2007. American Psychological Association. Washington, DC. 4, 5, 17, 24, 45–46, 75, 76, 115, 132.

Silvia, Paul J. *Write It Up: Practical Strategies for Writing and Publishing Journal Articles*. 2014. American Psychological Association. Washington, DC.

ABOUT THE AUTHOR

Kimberly A. Skarupski, PhD, MPH is the Associate Dean for Faculty Development in the Office of Faculty Development and Associate Professor of Medicine (Division of Geriatric Medicine and Gerontology) in the School of Medicine and Associate Professor of Epidemiology in the Bloomberg School of Public Health at Johns Hopkins University.

Dr. Skarupski has started more than 100 WAGs for more than 500 faculty members and trainees across the schools of Medicine, Nursing, and Public Health at Johns Hopkins. She's given her WAGs talk to dozens of institutions and organizations, and has evidence of WAGs participants reporting great successes in establishing and sustaining good writing habits.

Dr. Skarupski has been focused on faculty development for 12 years and has expertise in leadership training, mentoring and coaching, and small group methods to increase scholarly productivity, build confidence, and foster community.

As a trained social gerontologist and program evaluator, the major theme running throughout Dr. Skarupski's 20+ year research career has been the quality of life in older adults, using data from large-scale epidemiologic studies to examine disparities in quality of life in this population, as well as the contribution of various social and psychological determinants of quality of life in older age.

Dr. Skarupski received her B.A. from Gannon University, an M.A. from the State University of New York (S.U.N.Y) at Buffalo, her Ph.D. from Case Western Reserve University, completed a post-doctoral fellowship at the University of Michigan and the VA HSR&D Field Program, and an M.P.H. from the University of Pittsburgh.

Learn more at **WAGYourWork.com**

Made in the USA
Columbia, SC
23 May 2018